DOMINOES

The Bird of Happiness and Other Wise Tales

LEVEL TWO   **700 HEADWORDS**

OXFORD
UNIVERSITY PRESS

Great Clarendon Street, Oxford, OX2 6DP, United Kingdom

Oxford University Press is a department of the University of Oxford.
It furthers the University's objective of excellence in research, scholarship,
and education by publishing worldwide. Oxford is a registered trade
mark of Oxford University Press in the UK and in certain other countries

© Oxford University Press 2011

The moral rights of the author have been asserted

2015 2014 2013 2012 2011
10 9 8 7 6 5 4 3 2 1

ISBN: 978 0 19 424919 5   Book
ISBN: 978 0 19 424917 1   Book and MultiROM Pack
MultiROM not available separately

Printed in China

This book is printed on paper from certified and well-managed sources

ACKNOWLEDGEMENTS

Illustrations by: Kristina Swarner
Cover Image: Kristina Swarner

DOMINOES

Series Editors: Bill Bowler and Sue Parminter

The Bird of Happiness and Other Wise Tales

Retold by Tim Herdon

Illustrated by Kristina Swarmer

Tim Herdon studied French and Italian at Oxford University before becoming an English language teacher, trainer and materials writer. He has worked mainly in England, Spain, and Japan, and now lives in England. In his free time he plays the piano and draws. He also enjoys reading, watching films, going to concerts, and travelling. He has adapted *Nicholas Nickleby* and *Typhoon* for Dominoes

OXFORD
UNIVERSITY PRESS

CONTENTS

BEFORE READING

1 **Match each title of a tale on the Contents page with a story summary.**

a A man without work saves an old man's life. The old man wants to give him a present, and shows him where he can find silver coins under the ground.

....

b An old man feels neither happy nor unhappy when good and bad things happen to him and his son...

c A boy becomes badly ill. His father makes him something that helps him feel happier and get better...

d A clever, beautiful woman finds answers to an important man's questions and wins his love...

e A poor young man decides to leave his village and become rich by selling something at the market. On the way, he tells everyone his plans.

....

f One man says that another man is stealing from him. The other man says that he is no A third man finds the answer to their problem...

g A boy finds a way to get a toy that he wants to play with by helping people.

....

h A young man tries to find the secret of making gold, and learns something about bananas from an older man...

2 **Match these people from the stories with the summaries in Activity 1.**

CHAPTER 1   The bird of happiness

A tale from Russia

A long time ago, a little boy called Igor lived with his mother and father in a small house which was made of wood. Igor's family was very poor. His father was a **woodcutter**, and his mother made clothes for rich people in the **city**. Their house was in the middle of a large **forest** in the north of Russia. In summer, the days were long and the forest was alive with the sounds of birds singing to each other. Igor's father taught him the names of the different birds, and the boy soon knew all their songs. But in winter, the days were very short, and there was deep snow everywhere. The forest **became** quiet because the birds left to spend the winter months in warmer countries.

woodcutter a man who cuts wood

city (*plural* **cities**) a big and important town

forest a place with lots of trees

become (*past* **became**, **become**) to begin to be

One winter, Igor became ill. His mother made special food and drink for him, but he only got worse. The doctor from the city came to see Igor, and spent some time talking with the boy, and looking at him. Then he spoke to Igor's mother and father.

'He's very ill, but I don't know what's wrong with him. This winter many young children all over the country are becoming ill and dying, and nobody knows why. I'm sorry but there's nothing that I can do to help. Give him lots of good things to eat, and make sure that he gets lots of sleep.'

During the next few days, Igor got worse. He became iller and iller. He spent all day in bed, and became bored with his **toys**. His father brought him little things from the forest to try to make him forget that he was ill, but he was not interested in anything. His face became white, and he didn't want to eat. Sometimes at night he had a **fever**, and then he **dreamt** that he was flying above the forest, looking at his family's little house far below him.

One morning, after a very bad night, Igor woke up and found his father looking at him.

'Is there anything that you want?' said his father.

'Yes, there is, Father,' said Igor. 'I miss the songs of the birds. Could you catch a bird and put it in a **cage** for me? If you put the cage above my bed, I can listen to the bird singing and remember the sounds of the forest.'

'Of course, little Igor,' said his father, smiling. 'I'll bring you your bird tomorrow.'

But he knew that, now it was winter, there were no birds in the forest. This was the only thing that his son wanted, and he could not give it to him.

'Perhaps you could make him a bird out of wood?' said Igor's mother. 'You could use one of those little pieces of wood that we usually burn on the fire.'

toy something that a child plays with

fever when you get very hot because you are ill

dream (*past* **dreamt** *or* **dreamed NAm Eng**) to see pictures in your head when you are sleeping; something that you would like to happen

cage an open box to put animals or birds in

It was a cold, snowy day, and the forest trees were hard to cut. But all day, while he was working, Igor's father thought about how to make his son a bird out of wood. 'Of course it'll never sing,' he said to himself, 'but perhaps if it's very beautiful, little Igor will like it just the same.'

After dinner that night, he started making the bird. The first few times that he tried were no good. The finished birds were all too fat and too heavy to fly. He put them one by one on the fire, and held his head in his hands. It was now the middle of the night, and outside more snow was falling. Then he suddenly said to himself, 'I know! The bird needs to be just two pieces of wood. If I cut the wood carefully, the bird can have real **feathers**.' First he took a piece of wood for the head, body and **tail**. He began with the tail, cutting the wood into feathers with his right hand. Then, with his left hand, he **smoothed out** the feathers. When he was happy with the tail, he took some more wood for the wings. He cut them out carefully. It all took a long time because sometimes the feathers broke and he had to start again. But in the end, he finished it. While the sun was beginning to come up, he showed the bird to his wife.

feathers birds have these on their bodies to keep them warm and to help them to fly

tail the long thing at the back of an animal's body

smooth out to make something lie flat

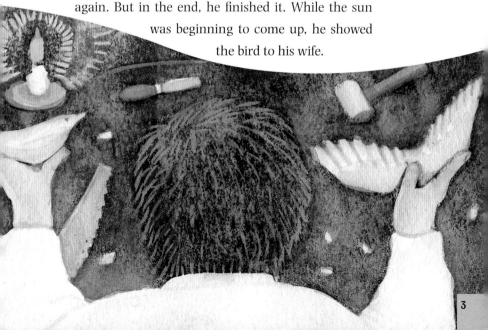

3

needle a very small, sharp, thin thing that you use to make clothes with

thread a long, thin piece of cotton

sew (*past* **sewed**, **sewn**) to join or fix pieces of cloth together to make things

tie to keep something in place with a string or thread

hang (*past* **hung**, **hung**) to tie or fix something at the top, leaving the bottom free

'It's beautiful, 'she said. 'But it's not ready yet,'

She took a **needle** and some **thread** and carefully **sewed** the ends of the tail-feathers and wing-feathers together. Soon the feathers were all together, just like on a real bird. Then she **tied** a long thread to the middle of the bird's back. This way they could **hang** it above Igor's bed. They looked at the bird together.

'Now that it's ready,' said the woodcutter, 'I'll take it into little Igor's room.'

Igor was asleep. Very quietly the father hung the bird above the boy's bed. He stood back and looked at it. The bird turned slowly on its thread. The woodcutter went happily to his bed to rest after his long night's work.

Later that morning, he went back into Igor's room. The bird was turning slowly above Igor's head. His son was watching the bird carefully. There was a light in his eyes for the first time in many weeks.

'It's beautiful, Father,' said Igor. 'Thank you. But I've never seen a bird like it before in the forest. What's it called?'

4

'That's a good question. I'll find out and tell you later.'

The next morning, when the woodcutter went into his son's room, he found the boy sitting up in bed, trying to touch the bird. 'The last time that Igor sat up in bed was many weeks ago,' he thought.

'So what's it called, Father?' the boy asked.

'I'm still not sure,' his father replied.

That night, Igor's father went into his son's room and he quietly made the thread a little shorter. Now the bird was hanging a little higher above Igor's head. Three days later, he found Igor **kneeling** on the bed, trying to touch the bird. His hand was very near it.

'Have you decided on the name of my bird, Father?' Igor asked.

'Not yet, my son. I'll tell you later,' his father replied.

Again the father went at night into his son's room and put the bird a little higher.

Five days later, Igor was standing on the bed, and nearly touching the bird.

'Father, help me. I want to make it go round,' he said.

'Go on trying. It's not as high as you think,' replied his father.

'And when will you tell me its name?'

'Very soon, my son,' replied the father.

Seven days later, Igor's father was cutting wood when he heard strange sounds coming from the house. He ran quickly to his son's bedroom. Igor was jumping up and down on his bed, laughing. Above his head the bird was going round very fast.

'Look, Father. I touched the bird!' shouted Igor happily. 'Now, please tell me. What's its name?'

'It's called the bird of **happiness**,' his father replied. And his mother, standing at the door, smiled to see her young son so full of life once more.

kneel (*past* **knelt**) to rest on your knees

happiness a happy feeling

READING CHECK

Order these sentences about *The bird of happiness*. Number them 1–11.

a ☐ Igor asks his father to catch a bird for him and to put it in a cage above his bed.

b ☐ Igor wants to touch the bird, but it is always a little too high for him.

c ☐ Igor is a little boy who lives in a small house with his father and mother.

d ☐ The mother sews the ends of the feathers together.

e ☐ Igor gets better and better, and at last he is well enough to touch the bird.

f ☐ The father spends all night making the bird for his son.

g ☐ Igor's father tells his son that it is called 'the bird of happiness'.

h ☐ The doctor visits, but doesn't know what is wrong with the little boy.

i ☐ Igor's mother tells her husband to make a bird out of wood.

j ☐ Igor's father hangs the bird above his son's bed.

k ☐ One winter, Igor becomes ill.

WORD WORK

1 Unjumble the letters to make words from the story.

a trafeeh   f. .feather...

b tefros   f. ....

c dutocotrew   w. ....

d paseshinp   h. ....

e mared   d. ....

f lenek   k. ....

g mecebo   b. ....

h vefre   f. ....

i hardet   t. ....

j yot   t. ....

Use words from Activity 1 in the correct form to complete the sentences.

a The ..woodcutter.. lived in the north of Russia with his wife and son.

b In winter, the .... was very quiet and there was snow everywhere.

c One winter, Igor .... ill and spent many days in bed.

d He had strange .... at night and didn't play with his ....

e The most difficult part of the bird to make was its ....

f Igor's mother sewed them together with ....

g Igor .... on his bed, trying to touch the bird.

h The 'bird of ....' made Igor feel better.

GUESS WHAT

The next story is called *The thief of smells*. Look at the people in it, and tick the boxes.

1

2

3

Who...	1	2	3
a ... is poor?	☐	☐	☐
b ... is angry?	☐	☐	☐
c ... is hungry?	☐	☐	☐
d ... wants to sleep?	☐	☐	☐
e ... doesn't like people?	☐	☐	☐
f ... wants to listen and understand?	☐	☐	☐
g ... makes and sells bread?	☐	☐	☐

A tale from America

baker a person who makes bread

customer a person who buys things in a shop

imagine to see pictures in your head

cake something that you eat on someone's birthday, after dinner, or with tea or coffee

delicious very good to eat

There was once a **baker** who had a shop in a small town in America. This baker was not a very kind man. He never gave his **customers** any more bread than necessary for their money, and he never smiled. But he was a very good baker. His bread was the softest bread that you could **imagine**. Sometimes customers paid for their bread and started eating it there in the shop. And his **cakes** ... mmmmm!! His cakes were really **delicious**. People came to his shop from all over town. When they walked down the street they smelled the baker's wonderful bread and his delicious cakes, and they walked right into his shop.

But not everyone came inside. Some people just stood outside the shop, smelling, and looking in through the windows. The baker didn't like this.

'Their stomachs are full of the smell of my bread. I'm giving them a free lunch! And I get nothing for my hard work,' he said to himself. 'Perhaps there's some way to put those delicious smells in bottles. Then I can sell them, just like I sell my bread.'

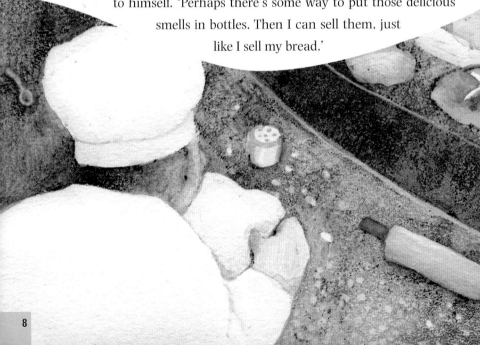

One winter morning, very early, the baker was in his shop, making bread. He wasn't singing happily while he worked. He was **complaining** to himself about getting up early, about the cold weather, and about anything that came into his head. In the middle of all this, he looked up and saw someone looking in through the window. It was a young man wearing an old coat. He was looking at the baker's bread and he was hungry. He was smelling the **fresh** bread and smiling. When the baker saw him, he felt very angry.

'That thief outside my shop has a stomach full of the smell of my bread! It's a free breakfast! I get nothing for my hard work, while he steals my smells.'

The man didn't move, he just stood there, closed his eyes, and smelt the fresh bread happily. The baker was really angry now. He walked across the shop, opened the door and shouted at the man, 'Pay me!'

'Pay you for what?' asked the young man in great surprise.

complain to say that you are unhappy or angry about something

fresh made not long ago, not old

9

'For the smells that you've stolen,' replied the baker.

'But I've stolen nothing. I'm only smelling the **air**. Air is free,' said the hungry young man.

'It's not free when it's full of the smells from my shop,' replied the baker. 'Pay me now, or I'll call the police.'

When the young man didn't pay, the baker took him by the coat and pulled him through the snow to the **judge's** house. He knocked on the door. After a long time, the judge opened the door in his night clothes. He looked at the baker and the hungry young man standing outside in the street. It was six o'clock in the morning. What could be so important so early in the day?

'This man is a thief. He stole the smells from my shop,' said the baker.

The judge was surprised. But all he said was, 'Come in and tell me your story. But first give me time to dress myself.'

He went back into the house. After a few minutes he came back, and he took them inside. They all sat down together round a large table.

'All right, tell me everything. Baker, you start,' said the judge.

He listened quietly. First the baker told him all about the hungry man who stole all his smells. The judge went on listening. Then the young man told him that air was free, and that any man could have as much as he wanted.

When they finished telling their stories, the judge was silent for a few minutes. The baker started telling him again of how the other man took all his smells without paying.

'Stop! Be quiet! I've decided what we'll do,' said the judge. 'Young man, do you have any money?'

The young man put his hand in his pocket and took out a few **coins**. He showed them to the judge, and said, 'Sir, this is all the money that I have in the world.'

air the space above and around things; we take this in through our mouth and nose

judge a person who says when something is right or wrong

coin metal money

'Give those coins to me,' said the judge.

The young man put them into the judge's hand.

'I've listened carefully to both your stories,' began the judge. 'It's true that the smells were coming out of the baker's shop. And these smells belonged to the baker. And it's also true that this young man took those smells without paying for them. And so I say that the young man has to pay the baker for the smells that he took.'

The baker smiled, perhaps for the very first time in his life. He held out his hand at once for the money. But the judge didn't give him the coins.

'Baker, listen and listen carefully,' he said. He shook the coins in his hands and they **clinked** together. 'That can pay for the smells,' he said to the baker.

'Give me my coins, sir,' said the baker, not smiling any more.

'No,' said the judge. 'I've decided that the sound of money is the best way to pay for the smell of bread.'

And with that, he gave the coins back to the poor young man and told him to go home.

clink to make the noise of metal things hitting each other

READING CHECK

The baker

The young man

The judge

1 Match the first and second parts of the sentences about *The thief of smells*.

a The baker wants to …

b The young man wants to …

c The judge wants to …

1 enjoy air because it is free.

2 make the young man pay with the sound of mon…

3 sell the smell of bread in bottles.

4 hear the stories of both men.

5 enjoy the smell of the bread.

6 get money from the young man.

2 What is *The thief of smells* about? Tick two sentences.

a Nothing in life is free. You must pay in some way for everything. ☐

b When you buy something you should pay only as much as you want to pay. ☐

c Don't complain about something that is too small to complain about. ☐

d The best things in life are free. ☐

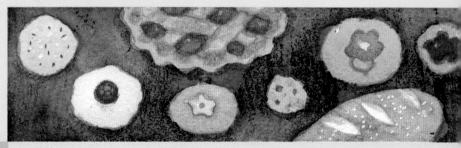

WORD WORK

Find seven more words from *The thief of smells* in the wordsquare.

Z	U	G	H	L	E	R	F	I	L	T
E	R	I	M	A	G	I	N	E	E	R
D	V	E	A	C	N	U	K	T	A	E
C	U	S	T	O	M	E	R	I	N	M
A	R	W	P	M	R	W	R	I	J	I
K	A	M	I	P	M	E	G	S	U	X
E	I	C	F	L	K	A	O	V	D	L
O	R	O	G	A	M	O	F	O	G	T
T	L	I	B	I	I	N	U	R	E	B
E	O	N	U	N	E	R	A	L	O	R

Complete the sentences with the correct form of the words from Activity 1.

a The ...... *baker* ...... put the fresh bread on the table.

b He .... a lot about his job and his life that morning.

c .... came to buy the baker's fresh bread and ....

d One poor young man enjoyed smelling the .... outside the shop.

e He .... the delicious taste of the bread, and he smiled.

f The .... made the young man pay with the sound of ....

GUESS WHAT

The next story, *The alchemist*, is from Burma. What happens in it? Tick the boxes.

	Yes	No
a The young man wants to become rich.	☐	☐
b The older man works for the young man.	☐	☐
c The young man sells lots of bananas in the market.	☐	☐
d The young woman helps the young man to become rich.	☐	☐

13

Chapter 3   The alchemist

A tale from Burma

problem a question that is not easy to answer

alchemist someone who tries to change inexpensive things into gold

dirt something dirty on the ground

Once there was an old man in Burma who had a daughter. He was very happy when she married a nice young man who came from a good family. At first everything went well, but after a little while there was a **problem**. The young husband wanted to be an **alchemist**. He spent all his time trying to turn **dirt** into gold. He was sure that this way they could one day be rich without working. Night and day he dreamt of finding the secret of the alchemists. He also spent a lot of money trying to find a way to make his dream come true. After some months like this, there was very little money. The young wife decided to talk to her husband.

'Husband, why don't you try to find a job? Trying to make us rich fast has left us with no money at all,' she said to him one day.

'But can't you see that I'm very near to finding the secret!' he replied. 'When I know how to turn dirt into gold, we'll be richer than you can ever imagine!'

Perhaps it was true that he was always very near to finding the secret. But he never found it. After many weeks, life became more and more difficult. Sometimes there were days when there was no money for food in the house. So the young wife went to talk to her father. The father was surprised to hear that his **son-in-law** wanted to be an alchemist. He asked to speak to the young man the next day.

son-in-law the man who is married to your daughter

father-in-law your wife's (or husband's) father

'My daughter has told me about your plans,' he said to his son-in-law. 'When I was young, I too wanted to be an alchemist!'

The younger man was very happy. Here, at last, was someone who could understand his dream. The **father-in-law** asked about the young man's work, and the two of them started talking about different ways of trying to turn dirt into gold. After two hours talking about the things that an alchemist must do, the old man jumped to his feet.

'You've done everything that I did when I was a young man!' he shouted. 'I'm sure you're very near to finding the great secret. But you need one more special thing to change dirt into gold, and I only learned about this a few days ago.'

'One more special thing?' asked the son-in-law. He found talking with the old man more and more interesting.

'Yes, that's right. But I'm too old to do this job,' he said. 'It's a lot of work and I can't do it now.'

'I can do it, Father-in-law!' shouted the young man.

'Hmm, perhaps you can,' said the old man. His voice was suddenly quiet. 'Listen carefully. The special thing is a silver **powder** that **grows** on the back of the leaves of the banana **plant**. This is a **magic** powder.'

'Magic powder?' asked the son-in-law. 'What do you mean?'

'Listen,' replied the older man. 'To get this powder you must plant bananas, lots of bananas. And you must plant them yourself. While you plant each banana **seed** you must say special magic words. Then when the plant grows, you'll see the magic silver powder on the leaves.'

'How much magic powder do we need?' the young man asked at once, very interestedly.

'One kilogram,' the old man replied.

'One kilogram! We'll need hundreds of banana plants for that!'

'Yes,' said the old man, 'and that's why I can't do the work myself, I'm afraid.'

'Don't worry!' said the young man, 'I'll do it!'

And so the old man taught his son-in-law the magic words and gave him **enough** money to start planting the bananas.

The next day, the young man bought a field. He planted the banana seeds just as the old man told him to do. He quietly said the magic words while each seed went into the ground. Each

powder something that is in very tiny pieces, like salt

grow (past **grew**, **grown**) to start to live; to get bigger or stronger

plant a small thing with leaves and sometimes with flowers

magic something that makes things happen in a way that you can't understand

seed a flower or tree comes from this

enough as much of something or as many things as you need

day he looked carefully at the little plants. He made sure that there were no banana flies on them. When the bananas came, he carefully took the silver powder off the banana leaves, and put it into a special bag. The banana plants grew quickly and the young man worked hard every day.

The only problem was that on each plant there was very little silver powder. So the young man had to buy more fields and plant more bananas. It took seven years, but at last the young man had one kilogram of silver powder. He ran to his father-in-law's house.

'I've got enough magic powder!' he shouted.

'Wonderful!' replied the old man. 'Now I can show you how to turn dirt into gold! But first your wife must come here. We need her too.'

When she arrived, the old man asked his daughter, 'While your husband was getting the banana powder, what did you do with the bananas?'

'I sold them in the market,' the daughter said. 'We've lived on that money for these seven years.'

'Did you save any money?' asked the father.

'Yes,' she replied.

'Can I see it?' asked the old man. So his daughter hurried home and came back with ten big bags. The old man opened them and saw that they were full of gold. He took all the coins out of one of the bags and put them on the floor. Then he took the banana powder and put it next to the gold.

'You see,' he said, turning to his son-in-law, 'you've changed dirt into gold! So you *are* an alchemist in a way, after all. And what's more, you're now a very rich man!'

READING CHECK

1 Correct seven more mistakes in the diary of the old man in *The alchemist*.

Today I showed my son-in-law how ~~poor~~ *rich* he has become. For seventeen years he has

planted bananas. He has looked after them very carefully, and he has kept all the silver

powder from the flowers. This morning he ran to my house shouting, 'I've got one kilogram

of the magic powder!' He was very sad. When my daughter arrived, I said I would show

them how to turn dirt into gold. While my son-in-law was getting all the 'magic powder'

all these years, my daughter bought all the bananas in the market. She showed us all the

money they had made – two big bags! Each bag was full of gold stones! I put the 'magic

powder' next to the gold on the table. All that gold really surprised my son-in-law! I said to

him, 'So you're an alchemist in a way, after all.' I hope now that he understands: there's

only one way to become rich. That's by working hard.

2 Are these sentences true or false? Tick the boxes.

		True	False
a	An alchemist tries to change gold into dirt.	☐	☐
b	The older man wants to help his daughter and son-in-law.	☐	☐
c	The young man is not really an alchemist.	☐	☐
d	He spends little time trying to make his dream come true.	☐	☐
e	The young man's wife wants him to find a job.	☐	☐
f	They plant many banana trees.	☐	☐
g	Each banana plant has a lot of powder on it.	☐	☐
h	The young man's wife sells the bananas in the market.	☐	☐
i	The silver powder from the banana plants makes them rich.	☐	☐

WORD WORK

Join the letters in the squares to make words that complete the young man's sentences from _The alchemist_.

a 'I said ....*magic*.... words as I put each
.... in the ground.'

b 'After a time the plants began to ....'

c 'I looked after each .... carefully.'

d 'I put the .... from the leaves in a bag.'

e 'I thought I could change .... into gold.'

f 'How hard it is to be an ....!'

alc	pow	rt	ow
ant	mi	ed	gic
der	di	gr	he
se	st	ma	pl

GUESS WHAT

The next story is from China. In it, different things happen to an old farmer. Are they good or bad?

		Good	Bad
a	His son comes home to help on the farm.	☐	☐
b	Their horse escapes.	☐	☐
c	The son finds a new horse to work on the farm.	☐	☐
d	The son breaks his leg.	☐	☐

CHAPTER 4   Good luck or bad luck?

A tale from China

A long time ago an old man lived in a small village in the mountains, in the middle of China. He had a son that he loved very much, but this son was a student in a city very far from his father's village. And so the old man lived and worked alone. Every day he worked for long hours on his **farm**. There was always a lot to do there. He was a kind, friendly man, and all the people in the village liked him. They knew that the old farmer needed the help of his son, a strong young man who was not afraid of hard work, but the old farmer never complained. The villagers often came over to the old man's house and told him how sorry they were that his son was not there to help him.

'When will your son come back home? It's bad luck for you to live alone, so far away from your only son,' they said.

But the old farmer always replied in the same words, 'Bad luck or good luck, who knows?'

One day, the old man's son came back to the village. The people in the village were very happy for the old man, and they all came to his house.

'Now that your son has come back, your house will be full of good luck again,' they said.

But the old farmer only smiled, and replied, 'Good luck or bad luck, who knows?'

People knew that the farmer was a man who used few words. They didn't ask him what he meant when he said things like this.

Life was hard in the village and nearly everybody there was poor. But the old farmer and his son were not as poor as some others. They had a horse, and on a farm a horse can do the work of four men. But one morning the farmer's son left the **stable** door open and the horse ran away. The son felt terrible.

farm a place in the country where people keep cows, sheep and other animals

stable a building where horses live

'What have I done? Work on the farm without a horse will be really hard. What will we do now?' he asked his father. And the people of the village again felt sorry for the old farmer and his son.

'This is very bad luck,' they all said.

But again the old farmer smiled quietly. He didn't look worried about the horse.

'Bad luck or good luck, who knows?' he said.

That afternoon some people in the village thought that they saw the old man's horse running across the hills near the farm. So that evening the son went to look for it. After a few hours he found their horse, quietly eating **grass** next to a wild horse. The son was able to bring both horses back to his father's farm. When the people of the village heard this news, they were very happy for the farmer.

'First you had one horse. Then you had no horse. Now you have two horses!' they shouted happily. 'Your good luck has come back again!'

But the old farmer just smiled his quiet smile and said, 'Good luck or bad luck, who knows?'

The son liked the new horse very much, and he decided to **tame** it.

grass it is green; gardens and fields have lots of it on the ground

tame to stop an animal being wild

21

'Be careful, son. You've lived in the city for many years. You don't know very much about taming wild horses,' said the old farmer worriedly.

'Don't worry, Father. I know what I'm doing,' replied the son. 'When I've tamed this horse, we'll have two horses to help us on the farm, and life will be better.' But the next day, the old man's son fell from the wild horse's back to the ground and broke his leg. Now this was a big problem. A man with a bad leg needs to eat, but cannot work.

Once again the people of the village came to the farmer's house to say how sorry they were.

'First your son was in the city and there was no one to help you. Then your son came back to help you. Now your son has broken his leg, and *you* must help *him*. Your bad luck has come back,' they said.

Once again the father smiled quietly and replied, 'Bad luck or good luck, who knows?'

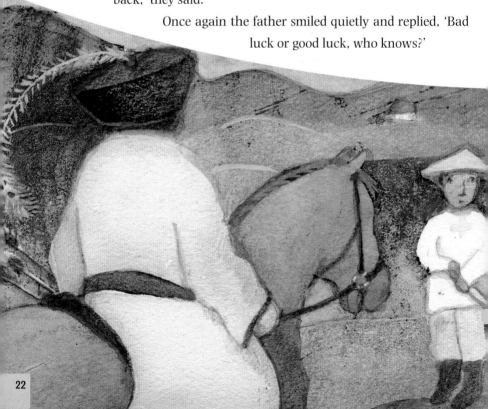

Some of the villagers were surprised to hear this. Where was the good luck in breaking your leg?

At that time in China, there was a long and terrible **war** between the east and west of the country. Every week hundreds of young men died in this war. One day some soldiers arrived in the village. They were looking for more men to fight with them. All the young men in the village had to become soldiers in the **army** and leave for the war. Their families cried when they said goodbye. They knew that many of these young men would be dead in a few days. But the soldiers left the old farmer's son behind. What good to an army was a soldier with a bad leg?

Now the villagers understood the old farmer's words. They went to see him.

'Your son didn't have to go with the soldiers because he broke his leg. It's true that your bad luck changed into good luck,' they said, happy that they understood the old farmer's **wise** words.

The old farmer smiled kindly at them.

'Good luck or bad luck, who knows?' he answered.

war fighting between countries or people

army a large number of people who fight for their country

wise intelligent, clever

ACTIVITIES

READING CHECK

1 **Match the two parts of the sentences about the story *Good luck or bad luck?*.**

a	The old man lives ...	**1**	because he works on his farm alone.
b	People feel sorry for him ...	**2**	are very lucky.
c	Things are easier when the son ...	**3**	with a wild horse.
d	But one day their horse escapes ...	**4**	the wild horse, but he breaks his leg.
e	They find the horse eating grass ...	**5**	in a small village in the mountains.
f	The son wants to tame ...	**6**	because he has a bad leg.
g	Some soldiers come looking ...	**7**	comes back from the city.
h	They leave the young man ...	**8**	'Good luck or bad luck, who knows?'
i	Everyone thinks that the old man and his son ...	**9**	for young men to go with them and fight in the army.
j	But the old man just says, ...	**10**	because the stable door is open.

2 **The old man in the story often says, 'Good luck or bad luck, who knows?' What does he mean? Tick one of the boxes.**

a Good luck is always really bad luck. ☐

b You often don't really know if something that happens to you is good or bad at first. ☐

c After good luck, you always have bad luck. ☐

WORD WORK

1 **Correct the underlined words in these sentences.**

a The old man's son lived in a <u>circle</u> far from the village...... *city* .....

b The son came back to help his father with the <u>factory</u>.................

c The son forgot to close the <u>station</u> door..................

d The horses were in the field, happily eating <u>glass</u>..................

e I'm going to <u>time</u> the horse and then it can help us on the farm..................

f Many soldiers died in the <u>car</u> and the army needed more young men..................

g In the end, the people of the village thought that the old man was very <u>wild</u>.

....

Match the words from Activity 1 with the pictures.

a c i t y

d t _ _ _

f w _

b f _ _ _

g s _ _ _ _ _

c w _ _ _ _

e g _ _ _ _

GUESS WHAT

The next story, *The basket of eggs*, is from Egypt. Here are two people from it. What happens in the story? Tick the boxes.

a Mousa is...

 1 ☐ taking eggs from his family's farm
   to the family shop.

 2 ☐ going to cook some eggs.

 3 ☐ going to sell some eggs in Cairo.

b His friend Abdullah is...

 1 ☐ going to buy chickens.

 2 ☐ going to help Mousa to cook eggs.

 3 ☐ giving Mousa some business ideas.

25

CHAPTER 5   The basket of eggs

A tale from Egypt

Mousa really didn't like being poor. He lived in a small house in a small village next to the River Nile in Egypt. When there was work, he worked on farms, and when there was no work, he watched the waters of the River Nile. Sometimes he dreamt that he was in a beautiful boat, going slowly up the river to Cairo. He dreamt of a new life there – a big house, lots of money, beautiful clothes and lots of food. One day, when there was no work and he was tired of looking at the Nile, he thought, 'Enough is enough.' He decided to leave for Cairo and become rich.

While he was walking down the street, he met his old friend Abdullah.

'Abdullah, I'm so happy to see you before I go,' he said.

'Before you go? Where are you going?' asked his friend, with great surprise.

'I'm going to Cairo to become rich,' replied Mousa, excitedly.

'How are you going to become rich?' asked his friend.

'I'm going to ...' Mousa began, but he wasn't really very sure of his plan.

'Listen, Mousa,' said Abdullah, putting his hand on his friend's arm. 'I'm going to help you. Come with me.'

Abdullah pulled Mousa down a little street, and took him to Hafsah's house. In front of the house there was a big garden with many chickens running around in it. Everyone knew that Hafsah's eggs were the best in the village.

'Good morning, Hafsah,' said Abdullah. 'We need two hundred eggs, in a big **basket**.'

'Why are we buying eggs?' asked Mousa.

'With these eggs, you can go to the big market in Cairo. There

basket an open box made from thin sticks that you use for carrying things in

you'll sell them for good money. Then you'll buy something else, and sell it in a different place for more money. You'll buy and sell, buy and sell, and soon you'll be rich. Then you can give me back the money for the eggs – and perhaps a little more for helping you to start your business.' Abdullah gave the eggs to Mousa, and they walked through more little streets until they came to the Nile. They found a boat which was going to Cairo.

'Here's some money for the journey. And Cairo is waiting for you! Good food, beautiful clothes, all the things that you've ever dreamt about. Good luck, Mousa. Come back rich!'

Mousa said goodbye to his friend and got on the boat.

Twenty minutes later, the boat left. In two hours he would be in Cairo, for the first time. A new life was waiting! Mousa closed his eyes and tried to imagine that great city.

'Mousa! Where are you going with all those eggs?'

Mousa opened his eyes to see who was talking to him. It was Khaled, the baker's son. He was going to Cairo that day to sell his father's cakes there.

'I'm going to Cairo to sell these eggs,' replied Mousa.

'Ah, like me. I take these cakes to Cairo three times a week,' said Khaled.

material clothes are made from this

'Well, no, not really. I'm not going to sell eggs all my life, you know. I'm going to be much more than that.'

'What are you going to do?' Khaled looked interested. A man and his wife from their home village also looked at Mousa, waiting to hear his answer. Mousa was very happy to tell them about his dreams.

'Well, first I'm going to sell these eggs in the market. I bought them from Hafsah, so I'll get good money for them.'

'Hafsah's eggs are the best in the village,' said Khaled.

'That's true,' said the man and his wife.

'Then I'm going to buy some beautiful **material**,' said Mousa. Some of the women sitting near looked at Mousa when he said this.

'And what material is that?' asked one of them.

'Ah, the finest material that you can imagine. There are materials in Cairo that you can't find anywhere else. Materials that are made with really beautiful colours ... I can't even tell you their names.'

The women looked at each other. One of them closed her eyes, trying to imagine those colours.

'I'll come back to our village and sell this material,' said Mousa. 'All the women will want to buy some to make new clothes, so I'll make more money.' Now all the women in the boat were listening to Mousa.

'With this money I'll buy a **ewe** and give her the best food to eat.' When he said that, a group of men looked at him.

'A ewe is a good animal to buy,' said one of them. 'You must give her apples sometimes.'

'Carrots are better,' said another man in the group.

'My ewe will eat both apples and carrots,' said Mousa. 'Later she'll have two **lambs**. I'll sell the lambs and their mother, and ... then do you know what I'll buy?'

Now everyone in the boat was listening to Mousa.

'A cow?'

'A boat?'

'A **camel**?'

'No, a **water buffalo**,' said Mousa in a loud voice.

'Ah yes, I see. From two hundred eggs to a water buffalo. That's good business,' said Khaled.

'Very good business!' they all said.

Mousa stood up excitedly.

'When the water buffalo has a **calf** I'll have two water buffaloes to sell,' he shouted. 'And after I sell them, I'll be rich. And when I'm rich, I'll have a **servant** to work for me. All day I'll shout at him, "Do this! Do that! Quickly! Run!" And if he's slow, I'll give him a big **kick**, like this!'

With that, Mousa kicked the basket of eggs and it fell off the boat into the waters of the Nile. Two hundred eggs went to the bottom of the river, and Mousa was left with nothing – only his dreams.

ewe a mother sheep

lamb a young sheep

camel a very large animal that people use for travelling across very dry country

water buffalo a big animal like a cow that people in some countries use on farms

calf a young cow or water buffalo

servant a person who works for someone rich

kick when you hit someone or something with your feet; to hit with your feet

READING CHECK

Choose the right words to finish each sentence about the story *The basket of egg*

a Mousa…

- [ ] **1** has a big house and lots of money.
- [ ] **2** had a big house and lots of money a long time ago.
- [x] **3** dreams of having a big house and lots of money.

b When Mousa first decides to go to Cairo to become rich, he…

- [ ] **1** has thought carefully about how to do this.
- [ ] **2** doesn't really have any plans for how to do this.
- [ ] **3** has many good plans for making money.

c Mousa and his friend Abdullah go to Hafsah's house to…

- [ ] **1** buy eggs.
- [ ] **2** buy chickens.
- [ ] **3** borrow money.

d With the two hundred eggs, Mousa is going to…

- [ ] **1** start a small shop.
- [ ] **2** buy and sell different things to make money.
- [ ] **3** start a chicken farm.

e On the boat to Cairo, Mousa meets Khaled, who is going to…

- [ ] **1** sell cakes at the market in Cairo.
- [ ] **2** buy and sell things to make money.
- [ ] **3** buy cakes at the market in Cairo.

f Mousa wants the other people on the boat to think that he…

- [ ] **1** is a rich man.
- [ ] **2** is clever at business.
- [ ] **3** has bad luck.

g Mousa kicks the eggs into the Nile…

- [ ] **1** by mistake.
- [ ] **2** because he has decided not to sell them after all.
- [ ] **3** because he is angry that he is so poor.

WORD WORK

These words don't match the pictures. Correct them.

a camel

..... ewe .....

b basket

....

c material

....

d calf

....

e servant

....

f ewe

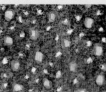

....

g lamb

....

h water buffalo

....

GUESS WHAT

The next story is from Mexico. The main characters are Mario, who has no job, and Pedro, the shopkeeper. Mark the boxes M (Mario) or P (Pedro).

Mario

Pedro

Who ...

a ... works very hard every day?

b ... believes that God will help him?

c ... helps an old man without thinking?

d ... only helps when he gets something back?

e ... suddenly becomes very rich?

f ... doesn't like sharing with other people?

CHAPTER 6 A gift of God

A tale from Mexico

It was six o'clock in the morning and – in his little house in a little village in Mexico – Mario was asleep. He was still asleep at seven, at eight, at nine, and at ten o'clock. Most days Mario woke up at about eleven. Then his wife usually went to the shop to buy **tortillas** and coffee for his breakfast.

Mario was a lucky man because Pedro, the **shopkeeper**, was a good friend and never asked him to pay for his food. But one morning, Pedro woke up feeling angry.

'I get up at five every morning to work,' he said to himself. 'But Mario lies in bed all morning doing nothing. He doesn't work and I give him free food. That's enough! If he wants any more free food, he'll have to do some work for me.'

Later that morning, Mario's wife walked into the shop at the usual time.

'Tell your husband that I can't give him any more free food,' Pedro said. 'I'm making an extra room on the side of my house. If he helps me carry some large **rocks** from the **quarry**, then you can have more food.'

tortilla a kind of very thin, round bread from Mexico

shopkeeper somebody who has a shop

rock a big stone

quarry a place where you get rocks from the ground

'Oh no!' said Mario, when he heard Pedro's words. 'Those rocks are too heavy for me to move. How many times must I say, "If **God** wants to give, He'll give. And when He gives, He'll push it in through the window." Please, no more talk of work. What about a nice cup of fresh coffee?' After that, he put on his clothes and left the house.

Later that morning, Mario was walking up the hill happily watching the clouds in the sky. Suddenly he heard shouts behind him, 'Whoa! Whoa, there!'

Turning round, he saw that a horse was **galloping** nearer and nearer. A man was riding the horse and shouting, but the horse didn't stop.

'Whoa!' the rider shouted again, but the horse didn't go any slower. Now the horse was right in front of Mario. He jumped at it, took the horse's **reins** in his hands and made it stop. The rider was an old man with long white hair. He got down.

God an important being who never dies and who decides what happens in the world

gallop to move fast (of a horse)

reins strings that are tied to a horse's head and that you pull to make it go one way or the other

'You don't run around all day like other people,' he said to Mario, 'but you're there when someone needs you.'

'You're very kind,' replied Mario. 'But to be like this is not hard. I try to sleep well, eat well, and not worry about things.'

'Well, today you really helped me,' said the old man. 'And so I want to give you a **gift** of God.'

'A gift of God? I don't understand,' said Mario.

'When God gives a gift to somebody,' the old man explained, 'only the person that God gives it to can keep it. Follow me.'

Mario followed him, and they went up the hill. There the old man stopped and showed him a large rock. 'Under that rock,' he said, 'are some leaves. Under the leaves are some **chests**. In the chests you'll find the gift of God waiting for you.'

Mario went over to the rock, knelt by it, and took it in his hands. He moved it easily. Then he moved the leaves, and saw six chests made of wood.

Slowly he opened one of the chests. Inside it there were hundreds of silver coins. He opened a second chest and a third ... all six chests were full of silver coins! Mario turned to thank the old man, but strangely he wasn't there any more.

Mario **picked up** some of the coins and put them in his pocket. Then he closed all six chests, put leaves over them again, and put back the rock. Now, after all this work, he felt tired. He sat down under a tree, and went to sleep.

When Mario woke up, he was hungry. He remembered something about a horse, an old man and some silver. 'Did it really happen or was it just a dream?' he said to himself. But then he remembered something much more important – lunch! He started walking quickly down the hill to his house. Suddenly he heard a clinking noise. He put his hand in his pocket and found six silver coins there.

gift something that you give to someone

chest a big box to put things in

pick up to take something in your hand

That evening Mario's wife went back to the shop. She put the coins in Pedro's hand.

'My husband sends you these. We need rice, a chicken, tortillas, tomatoes, and coffee.'

Pedro's mouth fell open when he saw the silver coins in his hand. 'How did Mario get so much money?' he asked.

'Come to our house tomorrow morning after eleven,' the wife said, 'and he'll tell you.'

The next morning Pedro heard the story. He wasn't really sure if it was true.

'But Mario,' he cried, 'why didn't you bring all those chests home with you?'

'They were too heavy,' Mario explained. 'I needed horses to carry them and I have no horses. And, my friend, how many times have I told you, "If God wants to give, He'll give. And when He gives, He'll push it in through the window."'

'I know!' Pedro said. 'I have some horses. I'll come to your house tonight and we'll go to this place together. My horses will carry all six chests; you'll keep three of them and give the other three to me. We'll become rich together! Do you agree?'

'All right,' said Mario. He was happy because his wife was cooking a delicious chicken for dinner.

Pedro went back to his shop. But he began to think, 'Why must I **share** the silver with Mario? The horses belong to me. Without them Mario can do nothing. And he won't know what to do with the money. He'll just eat and sleep as usual. But I always know what to do with money. I'll build a larger house ...'

That night, at eleven o'clock, Mario was asleep.

'Husband,' said his wife. 'Wake up. It's already eleven o'clock and your friend hasn't come.'

'He's just late,' said Mario and he went back to sleep.

An hour later the wife woke her husband again.

'Husband, it's midnight and I'm afraid that Pedro has decided to keep all the silver for himself.'

'Midnight? It's too late to go anywhere now. Wife, go to sleep.'

After that, Mario and his wife slept all through the night without waking up again.

While Mario was sleeping, Pedro went up the hill with his horses and his men. He told the men to move the rock and look under the leaves. They found the six chests. 'Open them!' Pedro said. But when they opened them, they saw no silver coins inside, only lots of dirt and stones.

'My friend Mario is laughing at me! He thinks that this is funny!' Pedro shouted. 'Well, I know how to be funny too!' He told his men to put the chests onto the horses, to carry them down the hill, and to leave all the dirt and stones in front of Mario's house. They did this, and then they went back home.

The next morning, when Mario's wife woke up, she couldn't open the door or window.

'Husband, wake up,' she said. 'There's something outside our house and we can't open the door or the window.'

share to take a part of something yourself, and to give the other part to another person or people

Mario got out of bed, and he pushed the door. He couldn't open it, not even a **crack**. He pushed the window, and at last it opened a crack. Lots of silver coins came through the crack and fell onto the floor.

'Husband,' the wife said, 'Pedro did come last night.'

'Perhaps,' replied Mario. 'But all this work has made me hungry. What about a nice tortilla?'

Later that morning, the shopkeeper's mouth fell open for the second time in two days. Mario's wife came into the shop and bought more food, and new clothes for herself and Mario. She put twenty silver coins down in front of the shopkeeper.

'What happened yesterday? We waited for you until midnight!' she said. 'I was worried when you didn't come. Then this morning it all came through the window. But surely you gave us more than half?'

'It wasn't me,' Pedro said quickly.

'Of course it was. Who else would leave all those silver coins outside our house?'

There was silence.

Then Pedro said quietly, 'Your husband always says that if God wants to give, He'll give. And that when He gives, He'll push it in through the window.'

crack a very narrow space between two things

READING CHECK

1 Match the people from the story _A gift of God_ with the sentences.

a Mario ...

b Mario's wife ...

c The shopkeeper ...

d The old man with white hair ...

1 has problems with his horse.

2 thinks that Mario never does anything.

3 cooks delicious food.

4 tries not to worry about things.

5 decides to keep all the silver coins for himself.

6 shows Mario six chests of silver because Mario helped him.

7 thinks that the shopkeeper will not share the money.

8 enjoys sleeping and eating good food more than anything.

2 Mario often says, 'If God wants to give, He'll give. And when He gives, He'll push it in through the window.' What does this mean?

  a Don't worry too much about life. If God is going to help you, you don't need to do anything. ☐

  b Only very few people get help from God. ☐

  c Don't ask why God does things in the way that He does. ☐

WORD WORK

1 Find words from _A gift of God_ in the coins.

Complete the sentences with the words from Activity 1. Show where each word goes.

a He lifted up the ⟨ and saw the

chests...... *rock* .....

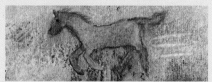

b When the horse began to, the rider

shouted, 'Whoa!' ....

c 'Why the silver with Mario?' thought

the shopkeeper.................

d They opened the door a and hundreds of

coins fell into the room.................

e Mario took the horse's and made

it stop.................

f 'If God gives you a , only you can keep it,'

said the old man.................

GUESS WHAT

The next story, from West Africa, is called _A wise woman_. In it, an African chief meets a woman called Zia. What do you think happens?

	Yes	No
a The chief marries Zia because she is wise and beautiful.	☐	☐
b The chief wants Zia to help find the answers to people's problems.	☐	☐
c The chief decides to kill Zia because she is so wise.	☐	☐
d The chief asks Zia to leave because she does not do what he asks.	☐	☐
e Zia leaves the chief's house, and he never sees her again.	☐	☐
f Zia leaves, but she cleverly makes the chief take her back.	☐	☐

Chapter 7   A wise woman

A tale from Guinea, West Africa

chief the most important person in a group of people, or a town

It was a beautiful African morning. Children were playing happily in the village streets. The women were washing clothes in the river and singing songs about lazy husbands. The great **chief** listened to the two men sitting in front of him.

'Great chief, the man next to me is a thief,' said the older man.

'Is that really so?' replied the great chief. 'Then tell me: what did he steal from you?'

'One of my sheep,' answered the old man.

'And what is your answer to that?' the great chief asked the younger man.

'Why steal sheep, great chief?' replied the young man. 'I have lots of them. If I need more sheep, I buy them. I don't steal them from other people. *He's* the thief, not me.'

The great chief looked at the far mountains and smiled. Then he looked at both men. Was the young one lying? He wasn't sure. But the old man didn't have the look of a thief. This was a difficult problem. He wasn't going to find the answer in

just a few minutes. But the great chief liked problems like this more than any other. It took some time to find the answer. People came to him from very far away to ask him to be the judge of their problems. The great chief liked this also.

solution the answer to a problem

sad not happy

'I have a question for both of you,' said the great chief. 'The person who finds the **solution** will keep the sheep. Go home and think about this question, and come back only when you know the answer. What's the fastest thing in the world? Don't come back until you have the solution.'

The two men left the great chief's house. The old man was **sad**. How could he find the answer to such a difficult question? When he got home he told the question to his daughter, Zia. She was a beautiful, happy woman who liked helping others. She was young, but she was also very wise.

'I know the answer, Father,' she said. 'It's "time".'

The old man went back to the great chief's house. The great chief was surprised.

41

'You're back again! Not even one hour has passed and you already have an answer to my question?'

'Yes, great chief,' replied the old man, 'it wasn't so difficult.'

'So tell me, what is the fastest thing in the world?'

'Time,' answered the old man. 'It always goes too fast. There's never enough time for all the things that we want to do. And when we want more time to do something, it goes faster.'

The great chief was surprised. The old man's answer was even better than his solution.

'Who helped you to find the answer? Who gave you these words?' asked the great chief.

'They're my words,' said the old man. 'No one helped me.'

'If that's not true, I'll **punish** you,' said the great chief.

The old man was too afraid to go on with his story. 'It was my daughter, Zia. She's a very wise young woman and she gave me the words,' he said.

'She must be very wise!' thought the great chief.

'Very well,' he said. 'You have found the answer and so you shall keep the sheep. And now that this is all finished, I think that I'd like to meet your daughter.'

The next day the old man brought his daughter Zia to meet the great chief. They sat at the great chief's table and had a big lunch – chicken, rice, fruit and a drink made from **palm juice**. During lunch they talked about the young man who stole the sheep, and about how difficult it was to be a good judge. The great chief enjoyed the lunch very much. While he talked about this and that with Zia, he felt so happy that he wanted to sing and dance. Was it the palm juice drink, or the wise and beautiful young woman looking into his eyes? But time always passes too fast, and soon it was time for them to leave.

The great chief saw Zia every day, and his love for her grew and grew.

punish to hurt someone because they have done something wrong

palm a tree with wide leaves that you find in hot countries

juice sweet water from fruit that you can drink

'You're a wise and beautiful woman. I'd really like to marry you,' he said.

'Me too,' replied Zia, laughing.

And so they married. The great chief was very happy, but he was also worried about having a wise wife. He didn't want her to help him with the problems that people brought him. He liked being the great chief who was a wise judge. He didn't want people to start talking about the great chief's very wise wife.

'Everything in my house belongs to you,' he said to her the day after they were married. 'But I ask only one thing from you. Never try to help with the problems that people bring me. If you do, you'll stop being my wife. I'm saying this to you only once.' Zia listened without looking at the great chief. When he finished, she smiled.

Zia and her husband were happy and life went well for a time. The great chief listened to people's problems as before. Zia was busy with the house and the animals. In the evenings he told her about the problems of the day and she usually agreed with his answers.

But one day two little boys went to see the great chief about a cow. Each boy said that it was his cow. The great chief gave them a very difficult question to answer. Zia knew which boy was telling the **truth**, because she often saw him in the fields with the family's cow. When he walked past her that afternoon, he was crying. Zia spoke to him.

'Tell me, little boy, what's the matter?' she asked him.

'The great chief gave us a question that I can never answer,' he said sadly.

'What did he ask you?'

'His question was: what's the biggest thing in the world?'

Zia knew that she mustn't help the boy. But the answer was easy for her and very difficult for him. And he was telling the truth about the cow.

'Go back to the great chief now,' said Zia. 'Tell him the answer in these words: "It is air. Air is all around us. When we walk, in front of us there is only air and more air. When we look up at the sky, there is air as far as we can see."'

The little boy went to see the great chief. He said the same words that Zia told him. This time the great chief wasn't surprised, he was very angry.

'Who helped you find this answer?' he shouted. 'These words are too wise for a young boy. Who gave them to you?'

'They're my words, great chief,' said the boy. 'No one helped me to find the answer.'

'If this isn't the truth, I'll punish you,' said the great chief.

The boy was afraid. 'It was your wife, Zia,' he said in the end.

The great chief was very angry with his wife. That evening he spoke to her.

'Didn't I tell you that everything which I have belongs to you? You have done the one thing, the only thing that I asked you

truth what is true

not to do. Now, take what belongs to you and go back to your father's home.'

'Before I go, can I make you one last meal?' asked the woman. 'Then I'll take what belongs to me and go.'

'Yes,' answered the great chief. 'Make what you want to eat. Take what you want to take. Just be sure that you're not still here tomorrow!'

Zia cooked the great chief's favourite meal: chicken with rice and vegetables. While he ate, she gave him a strong drink made from palm juice. She gave him many cups of it. At the end of the meal, the great chief lay down and slept.

With her family's help, Zia carried the great chief to her father's home. They put him on a bed, and he stayed in a deep sleep all night.

In the morning a great voice woke everyone in the house.

'Where am I? What am I doing here?' shouted the great chief.

Zia ran into the room, laughing.

'You said that I could take anything that I wanted from your house. I wanted you and so I took you.'

'You are truly wise,' smiled the great chief. 'Come, let's go back to our home together. Only a stupid man would send away so wise a woman.'

'And you, my great chief, are not a stupid man,' said his clever wife.

READING CHECK

Circle the correct words to complete each sentence.

a Two men come to see the great chief because
they want to sell him a sheep / *each man says that the sheep belongs to him.*

b The chief finds the answers to problems between people by
giving them difficult questions to answer / *looking at the people carefully.*

c The old man is sad because he doesn't have *a son, only a daughter* /
an answer to the chief's question.

d Zia says that the fastest thing in the world is *light* / *time.*

e The chief wants to meet Zia because he *thinks that she must be very wise* /
wants to punish her.

f The chief falls in love with Zia because she *cooks very well* / *is wise and beautiful.*

g The chief is worried that people will *like Zia more* / *think that Zia is wiser than him.*

h The chief tells Zia *always to agree with him* /
never to help with the problems that people bring him.

i Zia says that the biggest thing in the world is *air* / *our dreams.*

j The chief is angry with Zia because she *helps a little boy* /
takes something that belongs to him.

k He says that she must go back to her house and take *what belongs to her* /
her money from his house.

l Zia chooses to take *the bed* / *the chief himself* back to her house.

WORD WORK

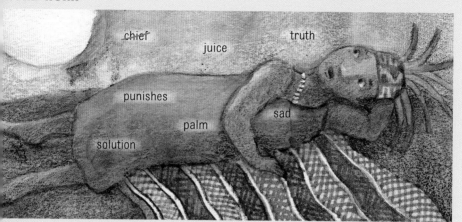

chief

juice

truth

punishes

sad

palm

solution

Use the words in the picture to answer the questions.

a Who do people come to with their problems? The ..... *chief* ......

b What does the chief try to find out? The ....

c What does the chief do if you do something bad? He .... you.

d How do you feel when a friend dies? You feel ....

e What do you call the sweet water from an orange? Orange ....

f What trees can you find in hot countries? .... trees.

g What do you need when something makes your life hard? A ....

GUESS WHAT

The next story, from India, is called *The drum*. The people in it need different things. Match the people with the things.

1 A mother who has a hungry little boy

2 A man and wife who wash clothes

3 A young boy who wants a toy

4 A man who has no shirt

5 An old woman who wants to cook something

6 A bridegroom who is late for his wedding

a a big pot to boil water in

b a horse to ride

c a piece of wood to burn

d some bread to eat

e a coat to wear

f a drum to play with

CHAPTER 8 The drum

A tale from India

grain it comes from a plant and people make flour with it

drum you play music on this by hitting it with your hand or a stick

flour we make bread with this powder

Once, a poor woman from India had a son. His name was Ravi. She worked hard making bread for rich families. They paid her with a little **grain** and she and Ravi lived on it. But she never had any money to buy nice things.

One morning she had some grain to sell in the market. When she was leaving, she said to her son, 'Today we'll have some money. Do you want something from the market?' Ravi knew that they had very little money and usually he never asked for anything. But that morning he said, 'A **drum**!'

The mother said nothing. She knew that she wouldn't have enough money for a drum. She went to the market and sold the grain. Then she bought some **flour** and salt to make bread. She felt sad that she had nothing for Ravi. So when she saw a piece of wood on the road, she picked it up and brought it home. She was sure that Ravi would find something to do with it.

Ravi didn't know what to do with it. But he didn't want to **disappoint** his mother, so he carried the wood with him when he went to look for his friends. While he was walking along the street, Ravi saw an old woman. She was trying to light a fire, and she was crying.

'What's the matter?' he asked.

'I need to make bread, but I can't light this fire. This wood is too wet,' she replied.

'I've got some dry wood that you can use,' said Ravi.

The old woman took Ravi's wood, lit the fire with it, made some bread, and gave a piece of it to Ravi.

Ravi wasn't hungry. But to say no to the old woman wouldn't be kind. So he took the bread and walked on. A little later he came to a young woman by the road with a child in her arms. The child was crying loudly. The young woman's face was tired and sad.

'Why is your son crying?' Ravi asked.

'He's hungry and I have nothing to give him,' the young woman replied.

Ravi gave his piece of bread to the child. 'Eat this,' he said.

The little boy stopped crying, took it quickly, ate it, and smiled.

'Thank you. You're very kind,' the mother said. 'Please take this **pot**. You'll think of some way to use it, I'm sure.'

Ravi didn't know what to do with a pot. But to **refuse** would be hurtful, so he took it and started walking again.

A little while later, he came to the river, where he saw a man and his wife. They were standing next to some clothes and a pot which lay in pieces on the ground. The man was shouting at his wife, and they were both angry.

'Why are you shouting at your wife?' Ravi asked the man.

'She's broken our pot,' he replied.

'I dropped it. It was a mistake,' said the wife, crying.

disappoint to make someone sad when we don't do what they want

pot people put water in this or cook in it

refuse to say no to something

49

'Perhaps,' the man went on, 'but people pay us to wash their clothes and now we don't have anything to **boil** water in.'

Ravi said, 'Look, I don't need my pot. Please take that.'

The man and his wife were very happy with their new pot.

The man took off his coat. 'You've been very kind. I want to thank you. Please take this coat.'

It was a fine coat, but it was too big for Ravi. He didn't know what to do. But he didn't want to disappoint the man, so he took the coat and went on walking along by the river.

After a short time, he came to a bridge, where he saw something strange. A man was sitting on a horse wearing only trousers. He was **shivering**.

'What happened?" Ravi asked.

'I was coming to the city on my horse. Some thieves were waiting on the road. They took everything – my money, shirt, hat, and coat – even my shoes.'

'Please take my coat,' said the boy. The man took it.

'You're very kind,' he said. 'How can I pay you for what you've done?'

'I don't need paying,' Ravi replied. 'I'm happy to help you.'

'Well,' said the man. 'You've done a very kind thing. So I want to give you my horse.'

Ravi and his mother didn't have enough food for a horse at home. But he couldn't say no to the man. So he took the horse, and went across the bridge to the other side of the river. There he saw some people going to a **wedding**: a **bridegroom**, his family and some **musicians**. They were wearing beautiful clothes. But they were sitting sadly under a tree.

'Why are you all so sad?' Ravi asked them.

The bridegroom's father said, 'We need a horse for the bridegroom. The man with the horse hasn't come. And the bridegroom can't arrive on foot, because everyone will laugh at him. It's late now, and everybody's waiting for us.'

'Please take my horse,' said Ravi.

'Are you sure?' said the bridegroom.

'Yes,' said Ravi. 'I don't want it.'

So the bridegroom took the horse.

'You're very kind. Now we can go to the wedding. But how can I thank you?'

Ravi looked at one of the musicians.

'Well ... perhaps you can give me the drum that your musician is carrying.'

The bridegroom gave some money to the musician, and he took the drum from him and turned to Ravi.

'Is that all?' asked the bridegroom.

'Yes, thank you!' cried Ravi, taking the drum. And he ran home, **beating** it all the way.

wedding the time when two people marry

bridegroom a man on the day that he marries

musician a person who plays music

beat (*past* **beat**, **beaten**) to hit strongly

READING CHECK

1 **Who takes which things from Ravi in the story *The drum*? Which things do they gi**
him? Use the words in the table to make sentences.

~~The child's mother~~		the horse		a drum.
The man with no shirt		the big pot		a horse.
The old woman	**takes**	~~the bread~~	**and gives Ravi**	a coat.
The bridegroom		the piece of wood		~~a pot.~~
The man who washes clothes		the coat		some bre

a .The. child's. mother. **takes** .the. bread. **and gives Ravi** .a. pot......

b ....**takes** ....**and gives Ravi** ....

c ....**takes** ....**and gives Ravi** ....

d ....**takes** ....**and gives Ravi** ....

e ....**takes** ....**and gives Ravi** ....

2 **Put the sentences from Activity 1 in the correct order. Number them 1–5.**

3 **What do they say? Match the sentences with the people.**

a He's hungry and I have nothing to give him.

b They took everything – my money, shirt, hat and coat – even my shoes.

c ~~I dropped it. It was a mistake.~~

d This wood is too wet.

e Is that all?

1 The woman who washes clothes says: 'I. dropped. it. It. was. a. mistak

2 The mother with a small boy says:...

3 The old woman says:...

4 The bridegroom says:..

5 The man on the horse says:..

WORD WORK

Use the letters round the drum to make words from the story *The Drum* that match the definitions. You can use some letters more than once.

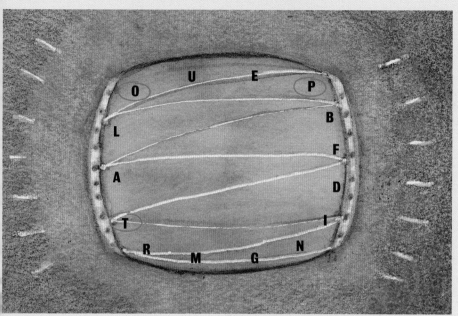

a POT – you can cook in this

b _ _ _ _ _ – you play music on this by hitting it with your hand

c _ _ _ _ – to hit strongly

d _ _ _ _ _ _ _ _ _ _ – a man on the day that he marries

e _ _ _ _ – to make water very hot

f _ _ _ _ _ _ – you can make bread with this powder

g _ _ _ _ _ – you make flour from this

Complete these sentences with other new words from *The drum* in the correct form.

a The people were going to a w edding.

b We felt d _ _ _ _ _ _ _ _ _ _ _ _ when they didn't come.

c The cold wind made us all s _ _ _ _ _ .

d We asked him to play football with us, but he r _ _ _ _ _ _ .

e All the different m _ _ _ _ _ _ _ _ played beautifully at the wedding.

Project A *Proverbs*

1 Match the proverbs about eggs with the pictures. Use a dictionary to help you.

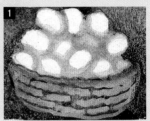  

a *You can't make an omelette without breaking eggs.* ☐

b *Don't put all your eggs in one basket.* ☐

c *Don't count your chickens before they're hatched.* ☐

2 The words in all these proverbs are about eggs, but the real meaning of each proverb is different. Match the meanings with the proverbs in activity 1.

i Will you have what you think you're going to have? You can't be sure until you really have it. ☐

ii Doing something new can bring you some problems, but this doesn't mean that you mustn't do it. ☐

iii Don't just make one plan for the future, because perhaps you'll lose everything if something goes wrong with that plan. ☐

Do any proverbs in your language mean the same? What are they?

3 Which two proverbs in Activity 2 match the main idea of the Egyptian tale *The basket of eggs*?

4 Use a dictionary to help you understand the words in these proverbs. Then choose the sentence that best explains the real meaning of each proverb.

a *Every cloud has a silver lining.*

1 ☐ If you want to know what is going to happen next, look carefully.

2 ☐ There's always a good side to bad things.

3 ☐ One bad thing usually comes after another.

b *Let the punishment fit the crime.*

   1 ☐ The way that you punish somebody must match their crime.

   2 ☐ You always know when you're doing something wrong.

   3 ☐ People who are criminals usually punish themselves.

c *Great oaks from little acorns grow.*

   1 ☐ If you want your dreams to come true, you must look after them.

   2 ☐ To do something very big you must start small.

   3 ☐ You have to wait for the best things in life.

d *You scratch my back and I'll scratch yours.*

   1 ☐ If you do something bad to me, I'll do the same to you.

   2 ☐ People like each other more and more as time passes.

   3 ☐ I'll help you if you help me.

Match the proverbs in Activity 4 with these four stories.

The alchemist ☐   *Good luck or bad luck?* ☐   *The drum* ☐   *The thief of smells* ☐

Here are some more proverbs. Match them with the pictures.

a *It's no use crying over spilt milk.* ☐

b *The grass is always greener on the other side of the fence.* ☐

c *You can't teach an old dog new tricks.* ☐

d *Don't put the cart before the horse.* ☐

Choose two proverbs from Activity 6. Use a dictionary. Answer these questions about them.

a What do the words mean? What does the proverb mean?

b Is there a proverb like this in your language? Can you translate it into English?

c Do you agree with the proverb?

Tell the other students in your class what you have found out about your proverbs.

Project B   *A Reading Maze*

A reading maze is a story in parts on different cards. To read it, you start with card 1 and choose the next part to read until you finish the maze.

1   This Reading Maze is about Mousa after the end of *The basket of eggs*. Which is the best/worst ending? Which is the shortest way through?

1   What can you do now that you've lost your basket of eggs in the Nile?
 a   Ask Khaled for money to take the boat back home.
 GO TO 2.
 b   Go on to Cairo.
 GO TO 3.

2   You ask Khaled for money. He says, 'OK, but you must help me sell my cakes at the market first.' What do you do?
 a   Say 'yes'.
 GO TO 4.
 b   Say 'no'.
 GO TO 6.

3   In the market square in Cairo people are listening to storytellers. What do you do?
 a   Sit and listen to a story.
 GO TO 7.
 b   Tell your story.
 GO TO 5.

4   You help to sell the cakes. Khaled puts money in your bag. There are storytellers in the market square. What do you do?
 a   Sit and listen to a story.
 GO TO 7.
 b   Tell your story.
 GO TO 5.
 c   Go home to your village.
 GO TO 9.

5   You tell your story and people pay you. You remember other stories and tell those too. Soon you have lots of money. You stay in Cairo as a storyteller. **You are at the end of the maze** and happy in Cairo. Well done!

6   You say 'no' to Khaled, How can you get home now? What do you do?
 a   Go on to Cairo.
 GO TO 3.
 b   Take money from a bag that you find.
 GO TO 10.

7   You sit and listen to a story. As you listen, a thief takes your bag. What do you do?
 a   Laugh, and tell people your story.
 GO TO 5.
 b   Go to the police.
 GO TO 8.

8 You go to the police. One of the policemen is Abdullah's brother. He gives you some money. What do you do?

   a Go back to the market square and tell your story.
   GO TO 5.

   b Go home to your village.
   GO TO 9.

9 With the money, you pay for the boat home. Abdullah isn't angry, but he says, 'You must work to pay me back.'

   You are at the end of the maze. It's OK, but what about your dream of making lots of money in Cairo? Do you want to try again?

10 You take money from the bag. It belongs to a rich man. He calls the police and they put you in prison. This is not the life that you wanted in Cairo. **You are at the end of the maze.** Better luck next time!

Here is the start of a Reading Maze about what happens to the old Chinese farmer after *Good luck or bad luck?* Complete the cards with the phrases from the box.

GO TO 2.   GO TO 3.   What do you do?
You agree that your son can marry her.   You tell your son that he can't marry her.

Your son wants to marry a young woman from the next village. What do you do?

   a Tell him, 'You can't.'

     ....

   b Tell him, 'You can.'

     ....

2 ....

.... His wife comes to live on your farm, and brings her mother with her. ....

   a Tell her mother to leave.
   GO TO 4.

   b Make sure that both women are happy in their new home.
   GO TO 5.

3 ....

.... He goes to the next village to marry and live with his wife and her mother. What do you do?

   a Write and ask your son to visit with his wife and mother-in-law.
   GO TO 6.

   b Go to the next village to visit your son.
   GO TO 7.

Write the first sentence of cards 4, 5, 6 and 7. What do you think happens in the rest of the maze?

4 Now write a complete Reading Maze. Finish the maze in activities 2–3, or write a maze starting with one of these situations. Follow the guidelines below.

What happens to Ravi after *The drum*:
One day a famous drummer comes to your village on his way to play for the king. Thieves have stolen his drum on the road. 'Have you got a drum that I can borrow?' he asks.

What happens to the young man after *The alchemist*:
You are now a rich banana farmer. One day a stranger arrives in town. He says, 'I am an alchemist. Give me some dirt and I can easily change it into gold.'

What happens to the baker after *The thief of smells*:
You are angry with the judge, but you go on working. You want to become rich from your bread and cakes. One day a traveller visits you. He tells you, 'I can put smells in bottles.'

Guidelines
- Write each part of the story on a different card.
- In the first sentence on each card, say what happens.
- Give two or more choices (a, b, c) of what to do.
- Show which numbered cards come next (GO TO ...).
- The maze should be between 10 and 20 cards long.
- Put good and bad luck in the maze to make it interesting.
- The maze should have different endings: good, OK, and bad.

5 When you finish writing your maze, other students can try it. Vote for the best maze

GRAMMAR CHECK

Present Perfect and Past Simple

We use the Present Perfect to talk about things happening at some time in the past without saying when.

? *'Have you seen this man before?' 'Yes, I have.'/'No, I haven't'.*

+ *'I've seen him outside my shop many times.'*

− *'I haven't worked for weeks.'*

We can put *never* between *have* and the past participle.

'I've never spoken to him.' (= at no time in the past)

We use the Past Simple to talk about things that happened at a specific time in the past and are now finished.

'When did you see him? I saw him yesterday.'

We often start a conversation about the general past using the Present Perfect, and then change to the Past Simple when we use a specific past time.

Complete the conversation between the judge, baker and poor man in *The thief of smells*. Use the Past Simple or Present Perfect of the verbs in brackets.

JUDGE: So, Baker, **a)** ..*have you talked*.. (you/talk) with this young man before?

BAKER: No, **b)** .... (I/not). But **c)** .... (he/be) outside my shop many times. He always comes and looks at my bread and cakes, smells them and goes away with his stomach full!

POOR MAN: But **d)** .... (I/never/do) anything wrong. Air is free after all, isn't it?

JUDGE: Please be quiet. **e)** .... (I/not ask) you to tell your story yet. Baker, what **f)** .... (he/do) this morning?

BAKER: g) .... (He/stand) at the window, stealing all my bread smells. Then **h)** .... (he/try) to walk away.
i) .... (I/stop) him and **j)** .... (I/tell) him to pay me.

JUDGE: Young man, is this true? **k)** .... (he/say) that to you?

POOR MAN: Yes, and **l)** .... (he/take) me by the coat and
m) .... (he/pull) me to your house. Sir, he's a bad man. In all my life **n)** .... (I/never/meet) another man like him.

GRAMMAR CHECK

Infinitive of purpose

We can use the *infinitive* to explain why we do something.

He bought a field to plant bananas.

2 Complete the sentences about *The alchemist* using the verbs in the box.

get	show	ask	have	tell
talk	~~find out~~	sell		

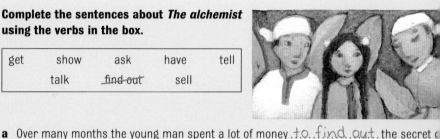

a Over many months the young man spent a lot of money .to. find. out. the secret (turning dirt into gold.

b His wife went to her father's house .... him for help.

c The old man went to his son-in-law's house .... about his dream.

d They needed hundreds of banana plants .... one kilogram of powder.

e The young man sat down in the field .... a short rest.

f His wife took the bananas to the market .... them.

g The young man ran to his father-in-law's house .... him the news.

h The old man put the gold next to the powder .... his son-in-law that he was now a rich man.

3 Match the questions with the correct answers.

a Why did the old man say that he was an alchemist when he was younger? [2]

b Why did the old man say that he needed one kilogram of magic powder? ☐

c Why did the young man say magic words when he planted the bananas? ☐

d Why did the young man look carefully at the banana leaves every day? ☐

e Why did they buy more fields? ☐

f Why did the father want his daughter to bring the money that she saved? ☐

1 To show it to his son-in-law.

2 To make his son-in-law think that he knew an important secret.

3 To make his son-in-law work hard.

4 To plant more trees in them.

5 To make the banana leaves magic.

6 To check that there were no banana flies on them

GRAMMAR CHECK

Echo questions

When we want to check what we have heard, or to show surprise or interest, we use short questions which 'echo' the subject and the auxiliary verb.

'Your life is hard without your son.' 'Is it?'   *'I can tame that horse.' 'Can you?'*

In the Present Simple or Past Simple, with verbs apart from *be*, *have got*, *can*, and *could*, we use do or did.

'You always look happy.' 'Do I?'   *'Your son left the stable open.' 'Did he?'*

Match the old farmer's 'echo questions' from *Good luck or bad luck?* with what the villagers say.

Could he?   Has he?   ~~Is it?~~   Won't it?   Does he?   Did he?   Do I?   Are you?   Were you?

a 'The weather's getting warmer.' ....'Is it?'....

b 'It won't rain for another two weeks.' ....

c 'We're worried that you can't do the work on the farm alone.' ....

d 'When your son was here he could do the work of five men.' ....

e 'You look so tired these days.' ....

f 'Good news! Your son has just arrived from the city.' ....

g 'We were thinking that he would never come back.' ....

h 'He had many problems on the road here.' ....

i 'He wants to help you on the farm.' ....

Now write the old farmer's 'echo questions' for his son's sentences.

a 'I was thinking of taming the wild horse.'
    ..'Were you?'..

b 'It can't be very difficult.' ....

c 'I'll start this afternoon.' ....

d 'I'm going to need two or three hours.'

    ....

e 'My friends can all tame horses.'

    ....

f 'They say that it's easy.' ....

g 'Ouch! The horse just kicked my leg!!'

    ....

GRAMMAR

GRAMMAR CHECK

Direct and reported speech

In direct speech, we give the words that people say.	In reported speech, we put the verb one step into the past.
'I want to become rich,' said Mousa.	*Mousa said that he wanted to become rich.*
'I'll walk with you to the boat,' said Abdullah.	*Abdullah said that he would walk with Mousa to the boat.*

We change personal pronouns and possessive adjectives in reported speech to match the speaker and the situation, too.

6 **Rewrite these direct speech sentences in reported speech.**

a 'I'm going to help you, Mousa,' said Abdullah.

..Abdullah said that he was going to help Mousa..............

b 'Mousa, with these eggs you can go to the big market in Cairo,' said Abdullah.

....

c 'I'm not going to sell eggs all my life,' Mousa told Khaled.

....

d 'There are materials in Cairo that you can't find anywhere else,' said Mousa.

....

e 'All the women in the village will want to buy the material,' said Mousa.

....

f 'Sometimes a good ewe has three or four lambs,' said a man on the boat.

....

g 'I'm imagining your life as a rich man with a servant,' Khaled told Mousa.

....

h 'I'll kick my servant to make him work faster,' shouted Mousa.

....

i 'I don't think that you're going to become rich with no eggs to sell,' Khaled told Mousa

....

GRAMMAR CHECK

Conditional sentences

We use *if* to talk about a possible situation in different ways. Here are two:

1 **if** clause + imperative **main clause**

     This is telling someone what to do.

'If Mario comes today, tell him he must pay for his food for last month.'

2 **if** clause + Present Simple + 'will' future **main clause**

     This is saying what the result will be.

'If he wants more from my shop, I'll tell him it's time to work for his food.'

When the *if* clause comes first in the sentence, we put a comma (,) after it.

Match the two parts of the sentences from *A gift of God* correctly.

a If you help me carry rocks from the quarry, ☐6

b If you move that rock, ☐

c If the chests are too heavy to carry alone, ☐

d If you come to our house tomorrow, ☐

e If God wants to give you something, ☐

f If you want me to wake you up, ☐

g If you can't open the door, ☐

1 ask a friend to help you.

2 He'll give it to you.

3 you'll find some chests under it.

4 tell me when you want to get up.

5 try to open the window.

6 I'll give you some more food.

7 Mario will tell you everything.

Write these *if* sentences in full.

a if/I/help/carry those rocks from the quarry/I/get/tired

     If I help carry those rocks from the quarry, I'll get tired.

b if/God/give/you a gift/it/be/only for you

     ....

c if/I/share/the money with Mario/he/not know/what to do with it

     ....

d if/I/not go/ up the hill with Pedro tonight/he/not find/the rock easily

     ....

e if/Pedro/open/the chests without you/he/take/all the silver coins for himself

     ....

GRAMMAR CHECK

Participle phrases

Sometimes we want to talk about two actions that happen at the same time.

'If I want more sheep, I don't steal them, I buy them,' he replied. He was smiling.

It is shorter, and more dramatic, to put a comma (,) after the first verb phrase and put the second verb in the –ing form just after it.

'If I want more sheep, I don't steal them, I buy them,' he replied, smiling.

9 **Change the following pairs of sentences from *A wise woman* in the same way as above.**

a 'What did he steal from you?' asked the great chief. He was looking at the far mountains.

........*'What did he steal from you?' asked the great chief,* ....*looking at the far mountains.*....

b The old man thought about the great chief's question. He was worried that it was too difficult for him.

....

c 'I know the answer to the question,' said Zia. She was smiling at her father.

....

d 'Who told you the answer?' asked the great chief. He looked very angry.

....

e The great chief looked into Zia's eyes. He enjoyed what he saw there.

....

f The little boy listened to the great chief's question. He was holding his head in his hand.

....

g 'That boy stole my cow,' said the little boy. He was looking at the other boy.

....

h 'Tell him that the answer is air. Air is all around us,' said Zia. She thought that this question was too difficult for the little boy.

....

i Zia walked down the street. She was singing happily to herself.

....

....

GRAMMAR CHECK

Past Simple: affirmative

We use the Past Simple to talk about finished actions in the past.
With regular verbs we usually add –ed/–d to the infinitive form.

She picked up the piece of wood.   *The little boy smiled at Ravi.*

With regular verbs that end in consonant + –y we change y to i and add –ed.

study – He studied at a little school in the village.

Some verbs are irregular. You must learn their past forms.

bring, give – She brought it home and gave it to Ravi.

Complete the sentences about *The drum* with the Past Simple form of the verbs in the box.

be	beat	boil	cry	drop	give	lie	
make	meet	shiver	start	stop	~~take~~	tell	thank

a Ravi .....took..... the piece of wood from his mother.

b He .... walking along the road to see his friends.

c He .... an old woman the wood to light her fire.

d The old woman .... some bread at once, happily.

e Ravi .... a young woman and her child.

f The boy .... because he .... hungry.

g With the bread in his hand, he .... crying.

h The man was angry because his wife .... the pot.

i The pot .... in pieces on the ground.

j They .... water to clean people's clothes in.

k The man had no shirt and he .... in the cold air.

l The bridegroom .... Ravi for the horse.

m Ravi .... his drum noisily on his way home.

n At home, he .... his mother the story of the drum.

DOMINOES
THE STRUCTURED APPROACH TO READING IN ENGLISH

Dominoes is an enjoyable series of illustrated classic and modern stories in four carefully graded language stages – from Starter to Three – which take learners from beginner to intermediate level.

Each *Domino* reader includes:

- **a good story** to read and enjoy
- **integrated activities** to develop reading skills and increase active vocabulary
- **personalized projects** to make the language and story themes more meaningful
- **seven pages of grammar activities** for consolidation.

Each *Domino* pack contains a reader, plus a MultiROM with:

- **a complete audio recording of the story**, fully dramatized to bring it to life
- **interactive activities** to offer further practice in reading and language skills and to consolidate learning.

If you liked this Level Two *Domino*, why not read these?

The Drive to Dubai
Julie Till

When his father is arrested in Dubai, Kareem has to move fast. He must show that his father is not a thief – and prove that his family is honest. For Kareem is going to marry the beautiful and intelligent Samira Al-Hussein, and she could never marry someone from a bad family.

So Kareem and his brother get to work quickly – with a little help from Samira.

Book ISBN: 978 0 19 424892 1
MultiROM Pack ISBN: 978 0 19 424844 0

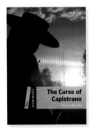

The Curse of Capistrano
Johnston McCulley

'Señor Zorro is on the road again, they say,' the landlord began.
'Why do I always hear his name?' cried Sergeant Gonzales angrily.

Zorro fights to help the poor and weak in California under the Spanish Governor's rule. Sergeant Gonzales has promised to catch and kill him, so how does Zorro always escape? And how will Señorita Lolita – the only daughter of a fine but poor old family – choose between Zorro, the exciting outlaw, and Don Diego, the rich but boring young man who wants to marry her?

Book ISBN: 978 0 19 424924 9
MultiROM Pack ISBN: 978 0 19 424923 2

You can find details and a full list of books in the *Dominoes* catalogue and Oxford English Language Teaching Catalogue, and on the website: www.oup.com/elt

Teachers: see www.oup.com/elt for a full range of online support, or consult your local office.

	CEF	Cambridge Exams	IELTS	TOEFL iBT	TOEIC
Starter	A1	YLE Movers	–	–	–
Level 1	A1–A2	YLE Flyers/KET	3.0	–	–
Level 2	A2–B1	KET-PET	3.0-4.0	–	–
Level 3	B1	PET	4.0	57-86	550